THE ART OF THE
ANCIENT EGYPTIANS
ART HISTORY BOOK

Children's Art Books

BABY PROFESSOR
EDUCATION KIDS

Speedy Publishing LLC
40 E. Main St. #1156
Newark, DE 19711
www.speedypublishing.com

In this book, we're going to talk about the art of Ancient Egypt. So, let's get right to it!

Much of what we know about the daily life of people in Ancient Egypt is because of the artwork they left in their tombs. It's unusual for the art of a civilization to remain relatively unchanged over thousands of years. The Ancient Egyptian civilization endured for over 3,000 years, but, surprisingly, their art didn't change much during that time period.

In their civilization, art was a representation of the divine principles in their religion. It wasn't meant just for art appreciation, but instead was a representation of everything they believed in. Their religious beliefs centered largely on the afterlife.

Egypt reliefs on walls in ancient temples.

THE CONNECTION BETWEEN ART AND RELIGION

Ancient Egyptian civilization lasted from between 3100 BC to 332 BC. In modern times, archaeologists found and continue to find their ancient art in Egyptian temples as well as in their tombs. The architecture of the temple or tomb was a form of art too. Inside each of these types of buildings were sculptures, paintings, and papyrus scrolls, which were early forms of books.

All of the art on the interior of the buildings was designed for two purposes. In the case of the temples, it was designed for the worship of the gods and goddesses highlighted in that temple. In the case of the tombs, it was designed to help the rulers, called Pharaohs, or other deceased people do well once they moved on to the afterlife. This type of art, which was designed to help people make a transition to the afterlife, is called funerary art because it was associated with funerals.

Egyptian Hieroglyphs: Medinat Habu, Luxor.

Ancient Egyptian Carving.

CHARACTERISTICS OF ANCIENT EGYPTIAN PAINTINGS

Egyptian paintings had a certain consistent style and you'll easily recognize it after you look at a few of the paintings.

When people are depicted in paintings, they are always shown at the side so that you see their profiles. The representations of people, animals, and objects in the paintings are always drawn as flat, two-dimensional pictures.

You can easily tell the social status of the people represented as well. The Pharaohs were the most important people, so they were always shown at a larger size than other people in the paintings. They were shown more like statues in their poses as well. They actually looked more like the statues of gods and goddesses than they did real people.

Sand-beige ancient Egypt wallpaper.

The ordinary citizens looked more relaxed in the paintings. Other people who had higher social standing were also shown larger in the paintings and in more formal poses.

Ancient Hieroglyphics.

Egyptian fresco.

CHARACTERISTICS OF ANCIENT EGYPTIAN SCULPTURES

The characteristics of Ancient Egyptian sculptures were very different than those shown in paintings.

The faces in sculptures were very realistic. Except for the funeral coffins, the bodies of people were always shown in an upright position, either sitting or standing tall. The poses are formal and not relaxed. Unlike the paintings, the faces are always shown full face in a forward position.

Men are shown with darker skin than women, possibly because they were outside in the hot Egyptian sun more than women were. If the sculpture showed a person who was seated, the person's hands were shown on top of his or her knees.

Osiride Statue of Ramesses III, Medinet Habu, Luxor, Egypt.

DETAILS AND COLORS

The Egyptians liked to show details in their art, but their art usually depicted ideal representations instead of exact duplicates of something they saw in reality. Their shapes were simple and well defined, set against a background of smooth color. The colors they used in their paintings were composed of mineral compounds and they have kept the vibrant look that they had when the paintings were originally created thousands of years ago.

Beautiful Egyptian Papyrus.

They generally used six different colors in their paintings and each had different symbolic meanings.

GREEN

The color green represented new life springing forth. For example, the god Osiris, who was the important god of the underworld, was often shown with green skin. Green was used as the color of re-birth.

Statue of ancient egypt deities Osiris and Isis with Horus.

BLACK

Black signified death, but it also represented resurrection to the afterlife. At times it was also used to represent fertility or life. Anubis, the god of the process of mummification was typically shown as a black jackal, which is a type of wild dog. It seems strange to us that a color associated with death could also mean fertility or life, but more than likely it was due to the black soil of the Nile that meant life and fertility to the Egyptians.

Egyptian statue, Anubis.

YELLOW

The color yellow represented the sun and therefore symbolized things that were eternal and couldn't be destroyed. Statues of the gods and goddesses were often painted a gold color or were made of gold.

RED

The color red represented anger, fire, and victory, which could have been for good or for evil. A person who acted with a heart that was red was filled up with rage.

Egypt hieroglyphs on a sargophagus.

BLUE

The color blue symbolized the water and the sky as well as the creation of the heavens and Earth. The important god Amon was shown with blue skin to signify that he was instrumental in the world's creation.

WHITE

The color white was associated with purity as well with things that were sacred in their simplicity.

Ancient Egyptian Painting.

Bas-relief at the Temple of Hatshepsut.

SYMBOLISM IN ANCIENT EGYPTIAN ART

Deeper meanings were behind many of the representations in Egyptian art. For example, the sun might be placed in a painting to represent creation or spiritual insight. Pictures were like codes to the Egyptians and each piece of code had layers of meaning.

The Egyptians also used different animals to connect specific qualities to their gods and goddesses. For example, the god Horus was painted with a falcon's head to show that he was a wise god.

Today, we don't have a very pleasant view of vultures, but the Ancient Egyptians admired vultures because they were known to nurture their offspring. Vulture headdresses were used to show maternal qualities.

Egypt: Temple of Kom Ombo.

The beetle or scarab was another common symbol that represented the power of transformation and persistence. Dung beetles used dung to lay their eggs and the young beetles would eat the dung and come forth to new life. The Egyptians used amulets, which were small charms or objects that were thought to have magical powers. Many of the amulets used in mummification had a symbol of the scarab to help the dead person get through his or her final judgment.

Sacred scarab in Temple of Karnak, Luxor, Egypt.

The Ankh was used to represent eternal life. It looks something like a cross but the top is a loop instead of a straight line. This important symbol is found in paintings and in scrolls and was a common amulet.

Symbols were so important to the Egyptians that their writing was based on pictures instead of an alphabet. This hieroglyphic writing has been deciphered by modern scholars and tells us much about the daily life of Ancient Egyptians.

Ancient Ankh Symbol.

Egypt panorama pyramids.

ANCIENT EGYPTIAN ARCHITECTURE

The Egyptians are known for their architectural marvel, the pyramid. Over 80 of the original pyramids are still standing today. These amazing works of artistic architecture also display the depth of mathematics and technology that the Egyptians understood.

The Great Pyramid was the tallest structure on Earth for over 4,000 years. It took over 20 years to build and contains over 2 million blocks of limestone covered with slabs of smooth limestone. The pyramids were burial chambers for Pharaohs.

Famous Sphinx and the great pyramids in Giza Valley.

Egyptian temples are also amazing feats of their architectural knowledge. One of the best known is Karnak, which is the oldest as well as largest ancient religious site in the world. It took several generations to construct. Its Hypostyle Hall is a great example of their architectural style. The temple at Abu Simbel is intriguing because it is carved directly out of the mountain. It has four massive statues that are seated at its entrance.

Hatshepsut Temple.

ANIMALS IN EGYPTIAN ART

Animals were important in Egyptian culture for many reasons. They provided both food and companionship. They were symbols and often represented characteristics of the gods and goddesses and were commonly used in art.

JACKALS

The jackal, a type of wild dog, is used frequently in their art. Anubis, one of the gods of the afterlife, was often depicted with the head of a jackal painted in the rich black that represented death.

CATS

The Egyptians adored cats. Cats were practical because they kept rodents away from their stores of grain, but they were also seen as somewhat magical. They were beloved pets and were sometimes mummified and placed in the tombs of their owners.

CROCODILES

The Egyptians feared crocodiles. The Nile crocodile still has a reputation as a man-eater. Crocodiles were frequently depicted in statues as well as drawings in temples.

Egyptian cat.

CATTLE

Egyptians prized cattle for both food and milk. They even used their feces to make fuel. Tomb paintings show cattle going through inspections and being milked.

Anubis jackal.

COBRAS

Cobras were frequently shown in the art of tombs and depicted in sacred amulets. The cobra was believed to be the Pharaoh's protector and the Pharaoh often wore a headdress with a uraeus, which was a stylized head of a cobra.

Awesome! Now you know more about the art of the Ancient Egyptian civilization. You can find more Art books from Baby Professor by searching the website of your favorite book retailer.

Made in the USA
Monee, IL
11 June 2024

59757244R00040